PITT POETRY SERIES

Nancy Krygowski and Jeffrey McDaniel, *Editors*

NO LONGER AT THIS ADDRESS

ANDREW HEMMERT

POEMS

Published by the University of Pittsburgh Press, Pittsburgh, Pa., 15260
Manufactured in the United States of America

Printed on acid-free paper

10 9 8 7 6 5 4 3 2 1

ISBN 13: 978-0-8229-6753-8

ISBN 10: 0-8229-6753-7

Cover design and book design by Alex Wolfe

CONTENTS

NO LONGER AT THIS ADDRESS

A LITTLE BIT OF HISTORY

Like an outdated telephone
I am always waiting
for someone to lift me
from my cradle and wrap themselves
in any correspondence. I no longer
have a cord, though once it was
the only way I ate. Little spaceman,
little stone. I am still incapable
of comparing myself to a gem,
but I loved amethyst as a kid,
and once bought some from the rock shop
in Breckenridge. They had also for sale,
in a thick glass display case,
the skull of a saber tooth tiger.
It yawned like a shipwreck
and devoured my attention
like so many cavemen   ·
and whatever foundational paintings
they never got to make. You
who have gone before us, today
I feel less musical than these crows
resting on their violins of electricity
running parallel to the roads.

I have never used a phone booth,
though like iron maidens
they still wait outside some gas stations
with the emptiest of arms.

LIKE STARS, LIKE SMALL-TOWN CHURCHES

When we drove up to Denver
to attend the inspection of a house

that would, ultimately, not work for us,
red-tailed hawks were everywhere—

staking out the light posts,
scouring the bit of prairie

between the Inn-And-Out Burger
and the community college.

They were probably after mice or rats
or whatever could be carried off

to feed their fresh-hatched chicks.
Or was it too far

into Fall for any new hawks
to adorn those high nests,

the likes of which sometimes miraculously
hang on long after

the fledglings have left?
The house was a nest of problems.

Garage too small
to accommodate a car and still

allow a person entry,
no radon mitigation, no overflow

valves in the bathrooms,
hallways too narrow for Karen's wheelchair.

And so as we went through
the litany of issues we were falling

out of love with it in real time,
the life we'd imagined living there

just blowing away, like how the dust
rose in wind from the in-progress interstate

we took there and back.
Most times I've made plans, reality

has carried them off,
though I am cursed

to be a planner, one who,
even if he knows the world

is a swirling current of indefinite seasons,
needs to impart some semblance

of control. Interstate, we do go on,
pitted by salt and overcommitted

to every direction under the sun.
The hawks were on the light posts

like traffic cameras, or like stars
above the cheap nativity scenes

of small-town churches
we passed on our way home.

IN THE MUSEUM OF RIP CURRENTS

In one frame a woman is inventing papyrus.
In another frame, rust has overtaken a field

of bluebird school buses. Take love,
for example, how like the tide it leaves

and returns, wearing down whatever it touches
until houses fall into the sea. In one frame

a three-headed cow is born,
what some people take to be a sign

of the apocalypse. In another frame the ocean
rears up like an impossible stallion.

In one frame a trickle of radiation
is pulled out to sea like a child

into a rip current. What we were urged to do
we ignored. I dedicate this wing to our new moon

which will not last, and which may
be a rocket booster from the sixties

falling back to earth. The challenge,
when riding those ancient buses, was to pry open

the stuck window so a breeze could enter you.

WILDERNESS AND THE AMERICAN MIND

I was thinking of a heavy hammer compelling
something molten and malleable into shape.
All this time, I've never gotten a clear answer
on Yellowstone, whether half of the country
is in danger of being buried under volcanic ash,
turned into another macabre garden
of statues like Pompeii. Play me something
on the jukebox, a little less reminiscent
of fire. Today our trees were wild
with blackbirds, thirty at least, all swarming
the feeders and picking dropped seed
off the ground. I figured they were just
migrating through until I remembered
how much of Colorado was burning,
and I realized the birds were probably fleeing
some forest crumbling into smoke. A neighborhood
cat came through the yard and sent the whole flock
tumbling up and away, a banished system
of shadows. I was thinking of a city
underground, one future posited by those
who think we'll ruin even the atmosphere,
make this planet scarred and unforgiving
as Mars. In Kentucky we climbed down

into Mammoth Cave, hundreds of feet
into the earth. The guide clicked off the light
so momentarily we were nowhere and bodiless,
how anyone would have felt lost in those sinkholes
hundreds of years ago. On our way back
to the world of light we found a bat
huddled sleeping against the wall of the staircase,
a solitary dark and folded heart.

NORTH AMERICAN BISON

For a beetle so loved the mountain pines,
the forests turned the color of a gunshot.

*

From the sky over Denver we could see
the Rockies burning, black carapace

of smoke clawing its way into the afternoon
storm clouds. The plane circled and circled,

visibility low, waiting for a chance
at the runway. We were flying back

from Florida, a place I had not yet come to imagine
as mine. Though I was born there. Though I was born

into a hurricane with my own name.
Below us on the ground the blue mustang

of Denver International Airport reared back forever
on its fading haunches—two fires, its inanimate eyes.

*

When Andrew tore through Miami, my father
left my mother and me in Orlando,

drove south with his coworkers
to join the relief effort. Distributed pallets

of canned water from the back of a rented moving truck,
toilet paper and MREs. Where the eye came ashore,

he tells me, there were quarters embedded
in the ruined cement, slingshot by the wind.

*

In Colorado, that year of fire,
the wind seemed to come down from the highest peaks

like a swarm of paper bats dreaming
of kindling, like a snarl, a prowling.

That was the year we went to the grave
of Buffalo Bill—its jumbled, simple stones,

its eternal, Western flame.

*

                              That was the year
my father climbed Mount Quandary alone,

snowboarded down until the snow
turned to mud. Trudged the rest of the way

on foot. He heard it in the distance
screaming warning—a mountain lion,

following him down through the melt off
and drowned grasses. When he finally broke

through the trees, touched two-lane highway,
there was no sign of his car, he had no idea

what direction was home. He flipped a coin
and started walking. Found his car a mile down the road.

*

Each time we drove into the mountains,
we passed a bison ranch. Once, we pulled over

and watched them meander their fenced-in field,
brown hills unto themselves. And a little later,

bison burgers at a tourist trap. In the gift shop
there was a toy cigar box that hissed

like a rattlesnake when I opened it, so loud
I dropped it on the floor and broke it.

*

Old train tracks ranged the dying, alpine forests
and we followed them over runoff streams,

prairie-fire and bluebonnet
piercing the rotten ties. A century earlier—

bison full of rifle shot collapsed
in bloody queues by the rails, routine as men

waiting for the train.

*

   There's no eternal flame
on Buffalo Bill's grave, though that's how

I remember it, tucked into that lonely pocket
of the foothills, fire danger high—

no eternal flame, though in the museum
dried specimens of flowers that once roamed

the mountains and prairies were displayed
like a miniature ghost town circus,

like extinct spectrums of light.

TO THE INSTRUMENT AT ARECIBO

When you collapsed, I heard
a researcher on the radio refer to you
as an instrument. What are your feelings
on music? Me, I think I would be a singer
if I had the talent. Songs will get stuck
in my head for days, the only way
I've been able to extricate myself from them
is by focusing on different songs. Somehow
they cancel each other out. Your message,
when decoded, shows the dimensions
of what the scientists referred to
as the average man. I think of them
walking your scaffolds like ants
on the body of a tarantula. Did you know
some spiders, at the end of each day,
eat their own webs and rebuild?
The researcher on the radio was doubtful
there would be enough funding to fix you.
Can you believe I first saw you in a movie?
Two spies were fist-fighting high in the air,
shoving each other again and again
against the balcony's cables, eventually
one threw the other back to earth.

We were meant to find this satisfying,
rewarding, and at the time I guess I did,
the way I used to love watching videos
of buildings being demolished. How things fall
in strata, almost. When I heard the sound
of you falling on the radio I could have sworn
it was the sound of a rocket taking off.

AS PER RAIN FALLING INTO WATER

Today's planned launch was scrubbed, bad weather
from Canaveral to Ireland, even briefly
a tornado warning in Brevard, though no funnel.
It's called a wall cloud, what comes down dark and hungry
out of the larger cyclone. One evening while I slept
in Carbondale, a tornado cut across a lake
ten miles south of my bed, sunk a shed's worth of tools
in that man-made body of water. Given a day's events,
talk about weather can seem banal or even
crude. So let me show you a hailstone the size
of a grapefruit, a trucker's windshield split open
with its falling. Or the hailstone is a helmet,
the only evidence of an astronaut's
disastrous return to earth. We fall sometimes
like dragons from heavens that wouldn't have us
without various incredible inventions
born out of the Cold War. You can invent
a lake and catfish will cling to the legs of herons—
like wet receipts, like ticks—in order to get there.

A DREAM OF GOLD, ETERNITY, AND CLOWNFISH

I was thinking of the gold in the cargo hold
of a sunken and undiscovered Spanish galleon.
I was thinking of the way Europeans ate
Egyptian mummies, how this explains
their rarity. They were buried brainless
and heartless, attended to by stone jars
containing their organs. I once wanted to believe
I could be pieced back together after death
with a halo or cybernetic attachments.
People freeze themselves still, hoping some day
they'll step back into the changed world changed—
their problems finally solvable, like waking
from a dream of your life into your life.
In last night's dream my father was walking
one of my dead dogs. I saw them through my windshield.
They stepped into the street and my brakes
wouldn't work, I woke up just as they rolled
over the hood. I was thinking of the way
I'm my brain, meaning I'm the one who creates
the dream that terrifies me to jolt and sweat.
Like I'm the ship full of stolen treasure
and the ocean it can't cross, the bones of sailors
disappearing into salt and the clownfish
shining like coins among ribs of coral.

HOW INEXTRICABLY AMOEBAS LOVE THE BODY

I was remembering a ferris wheel by a city river at night, turning
a neon roulette against that black and starless water. I was remembering
a bad harvest, and then an infestation in what little crop remained,
all the corn darkening with hunger and rot. There are some bugs
we consider allies—ladybugs, for example, eat aphids, and spiders
decorate their sails with the husked bodies of mosquitoes. Spider season
ends abruptly in Colorado, or what I've taken to calling spider season,
when for a few hot months wolves invade the basement and leave
their exoskeletons dotting the tan carpet, like abandoned military vehicles
in a desert. Halfway through August the wolves retreat and all
that's left are house spiders and the occasional ear wig. Was it a myth
that they'd crawl into your sleep and take up anchorage? I swam in warm water
in Florida, though I knew the risks, how inextricably amoebas
love the body, how inevitable their voyage to the center of the skull.
In Jules Verne's story the center of the earth is hollow, full of dinosaurs,
which as a paleontology-obsessed child I loved to imagine. In truth the center
is heat and crushing pressure, nothing could survive or escape it.
Not even the light of the stars that collapsed to create us. I think of them
like silos going bad, and us as insects drunk on their misfortune.

IF I HAD A TIME CAPSULE

There was a particular blue sheen
to the shadows, how the maples stood

in the way of the late sun.
In a few days, we'll take an hour

of daylight from the afternoon
and give it to the morning. As tribute,

or to make amends, but for what.
It was only recently I found out

the iron maiden was not historically used
as a form of torture, but was made up,

a modern approximation of the brutality
of the past. People want to live in the past

as if things were better then, but I wouldn't
choose watching the first moon landing

over having affordable health care.
Not that it's perfect, or even close.

I'm still waiting to be reimbursed
for teletherapy sessions I had

months ago. More specifically,
it's almost November. The pumpkins

put out last month on doorsteps
now sagging like leaking tires, the trees giving up

their leaves in earnest, some without
even turning sunset. Just piles of money

strewn over lawns and sidewalks.
Someone recently dumped their trash

on our street—two torn sweaters,
a hollow aluminum heart

that once held chocolates,
hard seltzer cans empty as wells.

If I had a time capsule I'd put into it
nothing, no guarantee

anyone will be around to dig it up.
Still I choose the future over the past.

Tomorrow, for example, there will
probably not be snow. I say this

all day to myself like a prayer.

THE ONLY RAIN

Life according to one article
might have originated on Mars.
But then again it might have originated
anywhere else. I like imagining
a comet passing through
like a garbage truck leaving
the building blocks of life strewn
in its wake. And yes this would mean
we were the collective refuse
of a cold and lonely stone.
The mountains on Mars
put ours to shame
but are bereft of trees
and therefore seem immaculate
in the way of famous cat burglars,
being known widely and also completely
unknown. Most things I've stolen
I've done so on accident,
a book I never returned, some clothes.
I've stolen anoles from outside
by way of not finding them
until too late, their petrified shapes
scattered like arrowheads

under dressers and beds.
I've stolen time. I am stolen time
in the sense that various things
could have already ended my life
but did not—car crashes,
gas station drugs, drunken swims
from pontoon boats and cliff jumps
into man-made lakes, lord knows
I don't take enough time to be thankful.
What do you do
with the knowledge that you missed
seeing a celestial event like Hale-Bopp
and won't ever get another chance?
The comet already light years from here,
having not ended the world
or taken anyone with it
away from the slow failure of the sun.
Though it was already too late,
I swept the crusted lizards
into a Mars-red dust pan
and carried them outside,
where the only rain was falling.

THE POWERPLANTS OF JUPITER

The animalia inherent to a cumulus sky
tracking seaward over a river lined

with morassed, red mangroves,
the lizard tenements of live oaks

older than St. Augustine shaking
pollen from their yellow-green vestments—

sometimes I have to imagine it back.
My brother says the pollen in Florida

is just as bad as ever. That's one thing
I don't miss, I told him. What I do miss

is everything else. Was remembering,
for example, sneaking out onto golf courses

after hours to fish the bass in duckweed ponds,
and counting the eyes of alligators

where they pierced yellow the surface
of the water. There's a picture of us

as kids in Cocoa Beach, smiling
wearing alligator foot necklaces

probably bought after an airboat ride
through retreating marshland, or after

visiting one of those interchangeable farms
to gawk at gators leaping for rotisserie chickens.

One thing I regret not doing in Michigan
was visiting the state's only alligator sanctuary

in Critchlow. I watched online
as new arrivals were named by poll,

donations requested for care—
some of the animals missing limbs

or slashed across the face, eyeless
from buckshot and arrowshot, the kind of thing

my high school friends joked about doing
at night on the chains of lakes. Myself

I never wanted a gun, except when I was a kid
and thought war a pastime. My parents tell me

as a toddler I pretended myself a builder.
I carried an L-shaped block, swung it

like a hammer. Then one day,
I turned it around and it became a pistol.

My dad has a gun somewhere in the house,
but I've never seen it. Which is my preference,

all good alligators never let themselves be seen
beyond the double glow of vision,

beyond the surrendered refuse of their bodies—
teeth on cords for kids to wear at Disney,

gator claw back scratchers, you get the idea.
The body as commodity, same impulse

that gave us freak shows, one of which
collapsed in Gibsonton, FL, where Lobster Boy

shot his daughter's fiancé to death.
Later, his own family put a price on his head.

When I drove there looking for more of the story,
all I found was an overgrown yard,

a kid's tricycle threaded with vines.
That town is circus murals

painted on the flanks of failing restaurants,
all-day happy hours, those who remain

propped up by the phosphate plant
on the other side of the salt-crowned Alafia River.

I used to cross that river every few weeks
on my way home from college—

home on an island that will disappear,
home I haven't been to in years,

the Alafia darkly sliding by like an animal
hungry for the powerplants of Jupiter.

LIKE THE POINTS OF COMPASS NEEDLES

Heat lightning, a tongueless dog.
Tonight the laws of America
pass through me like ozone.
A lawn mower sputters, cutting
through a yard thick with wildflowers.
All summer I watched them
going up in that grass, steeples
over nothing's chapel. Hail Mary
says the single green sprig
growing out of the cauterized stump.
There are some things I've attempted
to keep from springing back—
catgut, clover, dandelion,
a few distant names. Satellites
like the points of compass needles.
Easy on a cool evening to pretend
this road connects to whatever city
you love the most, whatever skyline
rises like a riverbank of cattails
behind the eyes. How the seed pods
break, then break into flight.

TO THE INSTRUMENT AT ARECIBO

I was reading about the animals
we've put into space. Monkeys and dogs

of course, but also spiders and beasts
so small you'd need a microscope to see them.

Spiders, in space, still figure out how
to weave their webs, though it takes them a minute,

and often the end result is wild
as a storm cloud, or a nebula.

And when a rocket crashed on the moon
last year, it was carrying thousands of water bears,

one of the most resilient creatures
we've yet discovered. Their faces bring to mind

a hybrid of a drill bit and a dinosaur,
and they will more than likely outlast us.

There's not many things that will outlast us,
I think. Alligators maybe, sentient driftwood

floating through flooded coastal cities. Some music,
hopefully, wherever collectors have hoarded

records away in basements or museum vaults.
I was reading an article about complacency,

how the frequency of so-called freak weather events
makes us numb to the worsening state

of this world we've created. How even the biggest storms
can collapse, dissipate into the larger onslaught

of the daily news. Instrument,
the researcher on the radio said Hurricane Maria

may have hastened your collapse. I flew
into San Juan a year after that storm

blew through, and the airport still wore the damage—
ceilings torn open, windows missing,

some terminals closed off and powerless.
We name hurricanes and they begin to feel

like individual offenders, like living things.

DEATH HAS A THOUSAND PICTURES IN THE WORLD

after a line by Brigit Pegeen Kelly

Of a common swallow. Of a common swallow
split open, and the beetle still ticking
in its stomach. Of a parking lot
where midnight children take their mothers' cars
and start up the mountain towards their bodies.
Of the Virgin Mary's portrait perched
on a cigarette display. Of a cigarette machine
with knobs like pinball, what catches the eye.
Of a stranger's smile like a hook and line.
A mange-broken fox shadowing its way
through hedgerows and bedding down in domestic,
pesticide-royal grass. Of pesticides
in garages, and pesticides in lungs.
Of the spider and her venom, that marriage.

WITH ARROWS THROUGH THEIR NECKS

Downtown the statue of a deer
was vandalized today, its flowering antlers
damaged so bad they had to be removed.
I don't know if we deserve art
or anything. My parents framed
a few of my middle school paintings,
have them hanging in the guest room
where I sleep when I come to visit.
Nowadays instead of painting
I accumulate useless coupons
and stray farther from anything
resembling stability. In my hometown,
people keep finding herons and cormorants
with arrows through their slender necks,
meaning there are critics
even of perfection. Here in the afternoons,
the storms slide down the mountains
and unload their complaints, hail
large enough to leave dents
in the grill out back, large enough
to total my friend's car. So what
if I'm happy for a moment
watching two birds whose names I don't know

fighting in the branches of a tree
whose name I don't know?
Anyone with information is asked
to step forward, into the light of day.

EATING HONEY FROM A CANOPIC JAR

In winter, honeybees gather around their queens and shiver
to keep them alive. Years ago the sky over the hollowed factory
was honey, sunlight combing through broken storms. No one yet
has explained satisfactorily why I so often dream of tornados,
or at least in those dreams I remember. All through Indiana
we drove in that weather to take your friend's wedding guests
to the airport, clouds roiling and surrounding, jaguars
of black smoke. Love is an atavism, or a dog in traffic.
I wasn't home when either of my dogs died, and I can't decide
if that's worse than the alternative. The pain, I mean.
One went during surgery in a doctor's office, asleep,
and one, nearly blind by then, fell into the pool at night.
The second time, my mother called to tell me while I was driving
and I saw the factory and the rain was barely falling
on the windshield. Often, when I dream of tornados,
those dogs are what I lose to the wind, again and again. Today,
despite the cold, the burn-purple wildflowers on the hillside
are livid with bees. I understand that under the right conditions
what they produce will never perish. I wanted to say,
what they love will never perish. The pain I mean.
Calyx and proboscis. How the subconscious seems to be
a strange, incessant catacomb of wings, needles, and warmth.

FIELD OF SUGAR

Things are vocational in heavy snow.
From the house's front step I can see

Christmas lights spreading out through the suburbs,
clashing like the colors bacteria

manifest in a petri dish. I tried
to imagine a world without tigers

and it felt like trying to imagine a world
without the color orange. Back inside,

football on the TV. I watch football
because I am in awe of what some men

can do with their bodies. Also the sound
reminds me of holidays at home,

the announcers and crowd collaborating
to match the clamor and height of the game—

the sound of it backgrounded as my family
gathered in the kitchen preparing the various

dishes that comprised our meal. Rare roast,
smoked fish dip, premade crescent rolls, our moment

in time. It's been a year since I've been back.
There are people who live their whole lives

thinking they belong elsewhere, or should have
been someone else, or will be someone else

after death. Today I discovered
my brown wingtips, the shoes I used to wear

to interviews, were full of cobwebs. Dust stuck
to the strands like a system of clotheslines

strung between the windows of two apartments.
To move from one job to another

like a hermit crab trying on different
ill-fitting homes. I remember holding out

my hand for a hermit crab, the class pet,
how it crawled aboard like I was a makeshift

driftwood raft, blunt legs clacking across
my open palm. I tried to imagine

the color orange without the world in it.
Once, on our way back from a school trip,

we filed off the bus to watch a field of sugarcane
burning. One farmer said they set the fires

to scare out animals, the snakes and rats
and rabbits, who lived there. Another farmer

laughed at this, for reasons I now understand.
The fire was fast, it was faster than I

had yet realized fire could be. Black shreds
of ash fell on us like flyers, like flies.

TWO CATS

And the heads of dandelions gradually
becoming wind, the way so many air balloons
fill the sky until they are the sky. Nearer to you,
oh Lord, and therefore more capable
of seeing your wounds, how they circumnavigate
your bright body like eyes. Some caterpillars
have evolved a resemblance to an altogether different animal
for protection. I have also, at certain points in my life,
pretended myself otherwise, stronger or more
in touch with my feelings, or with the violence
of my fists, which for some people
seems the only value of hands. Last night the cat
we walk with through the neighborhood was attacked
by a larger cat—she yowled and raced hissing past us.
We coaxed her out from under a pickup truck,
checked her for blood in the streetlights.
The college kids keep leaving their bottles in the road,
sometimes even throwing them against the asphalt
so that they become—nearer to you, oh Lord—
a strewn spike trap of green and amber stars.

TO THE INSTRUMENT AT ARECIBO

When I say a satellite dish is the opposite of an umbrella

When the dogs fall back out of orbit, distant fireflies shining at the edge of the abandoned orchard

When NASA announces a plan for retiring the ISS

When a drop of water spins in zero gravity like a shot warplane plummeting

When the warplanes wake me again

When I find the patches from my uncle commemorating different shuttle missions

When I first see a shuttle in a museum instead of on a launchpad, or fighting earth's barrier of fire in reentry—suspended in the room like the skeleton of a whale

When whales drift like nebulae

When I learn that nebulae also means clouds of the eye

When so much of the initial interest in space travel was driven by competition with communists

When the nuclear silos open to reveal descendants of such flight

When the nuclear silos open like derechos

When the nuclear silos open like graves

When I say a satellite dish is the opposite of an umbrella

SHOULD ALL OUR GREATNESS BE FORGOT

And now New Year's Eve again, this reminder that the world doesn't need us
to go on. The stoplights will keep changing and the drivers

will keep ignoring them, flooring it through the reds, the traffic cameras
will take their scandalous pictures until a strong enough storm

snaps them from their perches and sends them crashing to the blacktop.
For my money the blue jay is the bird with the greatest distance

between the beauty of its body and the ugliness of its song.
I hope to be the opposite of the jay, though most days I open my mouth

and statistics pour out like mudslides. I am wondering again
what subsequent disaster will be enough to end us.

Until then I have champagne, and gulf shrimp for a boil. Until then
there is the descent of the glittering man-made meteor into Times Square.

"Should all our greatness be forgot" is how I used to think
"Auld Lang Syne" went, I've sang a lot of songs I didn't really understand.

The stubborn morse code of Christmas lights beats red and green
against the evening. I am listening, I am listening for the sound

of something shifting in the air, though it's just our latest number
running its course. There's only so much you can do

with numbers. Whereas a song can show you a train trailing gray smoke
over the prairie in the last dusk of a number's world. I am trying

to unlearn my allegiance to numbers. I am trying to learn a kind of faith
despite my finite nature. I wanted to dedicate this to the man

who ran a red today and almost killed me. As I slammed on my brakes
and jolted against my seat belt like a crash test dummy in a trial run,

I could see him scrolling on his phone—just like me,
more a citizen of the internet than of physical experience.

That's how it feels anyways. I resolve to visualize the feeling
of standing in a cold river as my clothes fill up with what must be snowmelt,

at least here in Colorado. I resolve to get a little dirt under my fingernails
and leave it there, so that I can take a bit of this year

into the next one with me, little time capsule the color of rust.

OVERPRICED BOUTIQUE

How do I love the world? Distractedly,
like fallen leaves love the asphalt until
a good wind comes through and turns them tumbling
towards anything else. I spent the morning
mourning the murder of an activist
who protected butterflies from loggers.
Early wilderness advocates were caught
in the opposing bear traps of needing
to pacify the forest for the city,
and needing also to acknowledge
they were, each day, unbuilding a cathedral
with their saws. There is in development,
I suspect, a pill for that feeling.
And the weight of the last glacier's absence,
and the next mass shooting, a little closer
to wherever you take your body most
for granted. If my body is a temple,
it's been repurposed for that task. It was once
a bowling alley in a strip mall,
once a chain diner, once a boutique
overpriced and full of silver dresses
from distant sweatshops, cheap leather shoes.
I try to love the world remembering

each leather shoe was once an animal
opening its sovereign eyes on a field
of clover and crickets, for the first time.

I PLEDGE ALLEGIANCE TO THE HEART

I pledge allegiance to the heart—
not the empty aluminum heart

shaped like an ass and created
for holding chocolate, but the messy heart

full of blood and pathogens and incapable
of lasting long away from the body.

I pledge allegiance to the real heart
which fills with plaque and like a shark

cannot keep from moving and stay
alive. I pledge allegiance to the heart

of a great white shark, which accelerates
as the shark accelerates, rising like heat

from the depths and bursting against
the sea's surface with a mouthful of seal.

I pledge allegiance to the heart
of the seal which feeds and keeps

beating the heart of the shark. The heart
of a shark is small for its body,

meaning the heart is like an ant
carrying the wings of a monarch

butterfly. The heart is many chambered
like a pipe organ. Many chambered,

also meaning spacious, also meaning
there is enough room for you here,

even when it is cold out and the country
pumps with blood, here. I need

reminding some days how spacious
and fragile is the heart, a mine

floating on the ocean and primed
to explode at the slightest touch,

a mine deep in the mountain
where men inhale coal dust as if breathing

the shadow itself, a mine whose collapse
could be triggered by the slightest shift

of the earth. People fall into mineshafts
all the time, and some of them even survive,

and the heart I think is how daylight looks
when you've been so long underground,

when you've been allegiant to anger, to doubt
without even knowing it maybe, like I am

sometimes screaming in traffic or fast
in the teeth of what could have been

but wasn't. In Texas as a child I gave
the pledge daily, placed my hand

over my heart as if reaching for it,
as if making sure it was still there,

and this I think is necessary
for survival, pledging allegiance to the heart

so we do not forget it in its solitude,
in its cathedral of tissue, in its circuitry

of blood which is, despite the myth,
not once, not for a moment, blue.

DEMOLITION DERBY

What I love is the hope inherent,
how the drivers seek out the beat-down

cars, the ones everyone else has
already given up for scrap. They believe

every rust-worn and road-battered machine
has left in it one more victory,

one more ride. I do think some things
are meant to happen, but mostly human things,

small things. Larger things such as day
turning over into night, or how stars

explode into nothing, or are converted
by gravity into black holes,

meaning they become less than nothing—
these things are not meant to happen.

The human way is to vanish
from an understanding of your own name.

We want that drama, to think the end
of consciousness is the end

of something significant. A narrative
implies control. One car I saw

had an American flag spray-painted
on the side door. As the game went on

the flag was beaten into different shapes
of windfulness, and then eventually

the door came free from its frame,
flapping like torn fabric in a storm.

The game was a storm. The cars
were like storms, in that

they had names, though gradually
more unrecognizable, more alienated

from them. There is an anonymizing force
inherent in the game, how each blow

renders the body less itself.
But also there is meaning inherent in the smell

of oil leaking from the chassis,
and how the last car standing,

which today I am willing to say
in no uncertain words

that I love, is only a little less broken
than whatever other cars it outlived.

TO THE INSTRUMENT AT ARECIBO

Did you hear about our new moon?
Apparently it's a 60s era rocket booster
falling out of orbit. Today is supposed to be
the day it disintegrates, whatever pieces
having survived reentry scattered like coins
in the Pacific. Our first moon strikes me
as the jealous type, which seems right
given it sometimes wears a man's face.
Instrument, it took me a long time to learn
how to share. It took me a long time
to learn how to let anything go.
Lucia and I found entrails on the sidewalk
while out walking, what looked like
a freshly extricated heart and intestines.
A rabbit is the likely owner,
how they overpopulate the neighborhood,
easy targets for cats, hawks,
and coyotes. I used to lie awake
at night listening to the howling
of coyotes broken only by the howling
of trains. I lived in Illinois, between
a moonshine distillery and a river.
I live in Colorado now, and next month I'm moving
to Denver, where some childhood

version of myself watched the millennium
arrive on the television like so much space junk
returning. I had a plastic top hat. I had plastic toys.
I had a dog and she swam in mountain lakes
and went deaf from the microbes
that lived there. To live anywhere
is a miracle, given how much matter
simply doesn't get to be alive,
not even once. The rocket booster
wasn't alive even as it carried life
atop that controlled explosion
we call flight, we call the final frontier,
we call the only hope of survival.
Instrument, I haven't given up on the earth.
It took me a long time to learn
how to let anything go. I'm watching
for shooting stars tonight, which are
not stars but rocks and satellites,
burnt offerings falling at a speed
I'll never experience. What better thing
to wish on—that which burns so bright
you can't help but see the world different
in light of its brief and terminal return.

AFTER MOVING

In a room full of boxes, I am listening
to the rain falling on my roof for the first time.
It's March. Denver doesn't know
whether it wants to be spring. Or maybe
that's not the right way to say it.
Everywhere wants to be spring. Things bloom early
and hard frost drags the season back.
Here the birds start singing long before the sun
has shown any sliver of its arc. Here the birds are trying
to build a nest in a hole in the siding
above my back door. I chase them off,
but like shadows they wait
and return. It is impossible not to love them.
They are the color of roadside peaches.

TO LIVE ON MARS

On one hand, I am temporary in a temporary world.
On the other hand, there exists a fruit named passion

with purple skin, full of tart orange pulp
and green-black seeds that seem

almost cut from the earth, given the geode
character of their color. My new backyard

is mostly mud, with various refuse
scattered throughout—tennis balls, bricks,

crushed beer cans. A family of blue jays
lives in a frost-emptied bush

near the fence, screeching like snapped wood.
There were dogs here, you can see the holes

of stakes they were chained to.
Karen found a car window

buried in the ruined garden, crocus bulbs
haphazard all along the fence. Last week,

three feet of snow, and all the neighbors
worked together to dig out the cul-de-sac.

Full sun struck the drifts diamond.
I think I could live on Mars,

if I had to. I'm saying I'm not convinced
I'd give up the chance to escape,

if things came down to that. But sometimes
the world swells up around me like a flood,

like a season, and in those moments it feels like nothing
needs to signify anything else—not the light

through icicles, not the hulking, abandoned hawks nests
or the wind-shredded plastic bags flagging these trees

I've never seen in full leaf, never known
outside of winter. Outside the liquor store

I saw a man throw his change into the air.
He was smiling, the coins rained down

effortlessly, like little pieces of the junked heaven
we've sent into space as shield and myth.

And when the neighbor's dog runs into the fence
flushing doves from the yard,

when the kid next door does backflips
on her trampoline and becomes, for an instant,

an astronaut—who am I kidding,
how could I ever abandon a world like this?

PROTESTANT EPHEMERA

What is human in us, I suspect,
will never die. This, perhaps,
means everything else will.

All the grasses with my favorite names
are invasive, all the state birds
are leaving their appointed offices

for more fitting climates, and rats,
as always, are ubiquitous as night.
So what if I am afraid?

I remember, eighteen years old,
seeing a grey horse lying on its side
in a pasture by the intersection

of two interstates, not being
able to tell in the split second of driving by
whether its great chest was moving, and believing,

truly believing for a moment, that horse's life
was all that mattered in the world.
Not the transplanted storm-hungry grass

that held it, not the stiff and twisted thorns
of the fence that bisected my witness,
not where I was going or how long

it would take me to get there.
And whether there was a single laurel oak,
whether weeds in its shade,

whether that tree's branches were ever climbed
by anyone other than caterpillar, kudzu,
and the rain, good lord, on its way

down to the aquifer's scaffold
of sinkholes? It didn't matter.
And I know now the horse, also, didn't matter

to the post office in its slow disappearance,
didn't matter to the greenhouse gases,
didn't matter to the wars

that will outlast us. But you,
of all people, must understand me.
You with your heart made of tax returns,

church chimes, and grey horses.

WESTERN LOVE SONG REFUSING THE APOCALYPSE

For one, it's hard to believe the world could ever end
when you're sitting under a tree full of wild cherries

eating a seafood bouillabaisse while honeybees
buzz past your ears like allied biplanes on their way

to save you. In Santa Fe, New Mexico,
my mother drizzled olive oil on a sliced heirloom tomato,

seasoned it with kosher salt and black pepper,
then we ate while using her phone to identify

constellations. If you pointed the camera at the ground
the app would show you whatever stars

were shining on the other side of the world—
shapes that promise to return, to go on

even if we disappear from beneath them.
So it's not that I think we're invulnerable,

far from it. I just think the apocalypse is
an anthropocentric concept. The next morning

we had breakfast in a hole-in-the-wall café—
huevos rancheros, smothered burritos,

bitter coffee, heaven. And later the smell
of the farmer's market, green chiles turning over

on red coals, pork sausages frying on skillets. I swear
it cured my hangover. I bought a bag of yellow pears

on my friend's recommendation, and the old man
running the fruit stall handed me a black plum,

said you should try this, so I did. And then I bought a bag
of black plums. I sometimes get overwhelmed

by the sensation of taste coupled with the knowledge
of how far every ingredient has traveled

to become part of my meal, and the environmental cost
of that journey. Sometimes it feels the best thing we can do

is eat nothing and lie in bed waiting for one
of various fires to consume us, then let the world

become the world again. Last week
my friend woke to a layer of ash

on her roof. She lives closer to the wildfires than we do,
but even here the air was thick

with smoke. We could feel it in the backs of our throats,
like the prairie grasses disappearing into ozone

were gradually becoming us. Ours
is a neighborhood of lost dogs. The same vanished yorkie

has stared out of a photograph taped to the mailbox
for weeks now. He's wearing a blue bandana

with yellow stars, and thinking about it
can ruin me for an afternoon. We've returned

more than our share of escaped boxers
and labs, even once a pair of limping pit bulls

who were trailed by a group of kids trying
and failing to get them back. But people speed

through these streets, and I don't want to imagine
where that yorkie ended up. I don't want to

imagine what this place will look like in twenty years,
how much more of the wild, western expanse will be

hidden under suburbs. The houses go up so fast
they almost seem like the facades of houses,

just cardboard cutouts designed to make you feel
like nothing is left but the dreams of real estate agents.

If the west has a definition, it must be more
than the dust of a shrinking prairie

shook from the fur of a skittish coyote
crossing the parking lot of a sports bar.

When I went looking for my old house in Lone Tree,
I couldn't find it at first. I was searching

for the prairie that used to run parallel to that highway,
for the antelope that threaded those hills.

I should have known it would be gone,
swallowed up in the city's neon crawl

of strip malls and chain restaurants.
Like the jumping cholla cactus, the city's thirst

so unquenchable its needles grow right through your clothes,
reaching for the water under your skin.

Yesterday after sex Lucia and I went outside
to find the hose had been left on, flooding the yard

with water in a dry season, and a pigeon
was lying dead on the patio, its head bloody

where it hit the kitchen window. I do wonder
whether we really see what we're flying towards

at such speed. I said sorry, then buried the pigeon
in the yard, where a few of the birdfeeder's corn kernels

had sprouted green against the xeriscape.

TO THE INSTRUMENT AT ARECIBO

I wanted to tell you about seeing the second-to-last shuttle launch.
It was cold in Cape Canaveral that morning, cold for Florida at least,

and we sat in folding chairs wrapped in blankets, the air its own
wet garment against us. When the shuttle rose on its pillar of beach-grey smoke,

a crown of fire, it didn't feel final. There were plans for another
kind of spaceship, plans to go back to the moon, to Mars. I didn't know

it would be nine years before astronauts launched from Florida again,
or how emotional I'd get when it happened. I watched it

on the news from Colorado. Mostly I think the idea of Americans
dropping their differences and coming together in celebration

of such flight is a transparent dream, an oppressive myth.
But I almost believed it, watching that rocket go up and not explode

into meteors, go up and stay, I am not trying to be sentimental
but damn if it didn't stop me from worrying for a moment,

damn if it didn't fill me with something resembling hope. Dear instrument,
what would we even do if someone finally answered your message?

I used to paddle out onto the lake at night and watch the satellites
bisect the stars, watch the planes carry across the void like water striders,

and hearing the wind in the cattails, and hearing the traffic in the wind,
I felt unbroken. I felt like you must have felt some days,

a small and purposeful thing floating under heaven.

THE SENATOR

There's a little tree growing in the window well.
If I knew more about leaves maybe
I could tell you what kind, but as it stands
my flora identification skills are rusty.
There's rust, too, on the safety grate
covering the window well's opening.
At some point the tree won't have anywhere
else to go, and maybe it'll grow wide,
come to resemble its own caged forest.
I'm surprised it gets enough sunlight down there,
to be honest. To be honest I'm a little afraid
of sunlight. My dad gets growths cut off
regularly, and my younger brother has already had
skin cancer, too many days surfing
refusing sunscreen. I also used to
hate the stuff, the smell and feel of it,
would dress in long sleeves and pants
out on the water, wore a mask
to keep light off my face. Then later, in Michigan,
I literally couldn't get enough sun,
so many weeks in winter you just wouldn't see it
and the house felt like a pantry
someone had forgotten you inside of,

well past your own expiration date.
I tried a full-spectrum lamp, tried multivitamins,
but there's no replacing the real thing.
Spring in Michigan was like remembering
your true name, seeing through snow's artifice.
And when all the trees leafed back into full green,
nothing could hurt you, nothing
could even touch you. I don't live there
anymore. I live here, and the tree
in the window well seems like it's rooted
in an inch of dirt and stones,
though the roots must go deeper than that.
I've been thinking about what I'm rooted in,
what light that space allows me.
I know years ago my parents strollered me
through a park in central Florida
with a three-thousand-year-old bald cypress
named The Senator, at one time
the biggest bald cypress in the world.
A woman burned it to the ground one night,
having started a fire with Spanish moss and bark
so she could see more clearly
the crystal meth she was trying to smoke.

These things happen, except sometimes what burns
is a life, or just a pipe of illicit joy.
We can't choose what takes root chemically
in our brains. I still wake up tasting the smoke
of my last cigarette, that hungover morning
when I drove the pack over to a friend's house
and left it on her kitchen counter.
To deliver myself from temptation—deep roots,
shallow impulse control, etc. Maybe I'll climb down
into the well and dig up that tree, move it
into the yard where the sun is full
and rich and no one has put a grate over the sky,
not yet. It's really that much space we are given
to grow into, as into our names.

NO LONGER AT THIS ADDRESS

I put two letters back in the mailbox—
one soliciting money
for some Christian Appalachian mission,
the other advertising a three-by-five American flag
in exchange for a donation to whatever cause
I won't look into the envelope to discover.
Both are addressed to the woman who used to live here.
It's illegal I think, opening mail
if it's not addressed to you,
but I don't know exactly how illegal,
whether it measures up to theft or sits
somewhere in the realm of loitering or driving
with expired tags. The woman who used to live here
had three dogs. They're three of the main reasons
my backyard is so ravaged—spare grass, mud cracking
in that classic dried lakebed desert pattern.
The property is littered with toys, tennis balls, an archeological site
of rubber bones. I can picture the dogs
running back and forth from fence to fence,
ripping up flowers and weeds, sending crickets
flying. In the face of destruction
it's useful to keep a running list
of the good in things. Today's endorphins for example

were provided by three rabbits
playing tag behind my house in the falling snow
while I was doing the dishes. They paused to eat the few weeds
protruding from the growing drifts, then pounced
on each other, jumping high and kicking
and probably needing that joy to stay warm.
To me it looked more cold than fun,
and that's partially how I can tell I've been exiled
from the country of childhood for good.
But it's not so bad here
in the country of the rest of my life. Just look
at all these coupons, these offers.
Someone is always trying to reach me.

ACKNOWLEDGEMENTS

Many thanks to the editors of the magazines where these poems previously appeared, some in different forms.

Alaska Quarterly Review, "Western Love Song Refusing the Apocalypse"; *American Literary Review*, "Death Has a Thousand Pictures in the World"; *Cherry Tree*, "Field of Sugar"; *Colorado Review*, "With Arrows Through Their Necks"; *Copper Nickel*, "No Longer at This Address"; *Cortland Review*, "Like Stars, like Small-Town Churches"; *Gulf Coast*, "Eating Honey from a Canopic Jar"; *The Journal*, "How Inextricably Amoebas Love the Body" and "The Only Rain"; *Kenyon Review*, "A Little Bit of History"; *Lake Effect*, "Should All Our Greatness Be Forgot"; *McNeese Review*, "The Senator" and "Two Cats"; *Missouri Review*, "To the Instrument at Arecibo (I was reading about all the animals)," "To the Instrument at Arecibo (Did you hear about our new moon?)", and "To the Instrument at Arecibo (I wanted to tell you about seeing the second-to-last shuttle launch)"; *Nimrod International Journal*, "Like the Points of Compass Needles" and "To Live on Mars"; *North American Review*, "In the Museum of Rip Currents"; *Sixth Finch*, "Wilderness and the American Mind"; *South Dakota Review*, "To the Instrument at Arecibo (When I say a satellite dish is the opposite of an umbrella)"; *Waxwing*, "North American Bison," "The Powerplants of Jupiter," "Overpriced Boutique," and "I Pledge Allegiance to the Heart."

"Field of Sugar" first appeared in *Cherry Tree: A National Literary Journal @ Washington College*, Issue 9, 2023.

"With Arrows Through Their Necks" also appeared in *Verse Daily*.

"Western Love Song Refusing the Apocalypse" also appeared in Jane Hirschfield's Poets for Science Global Gallery (poetsforscience.org).